Genre Realistic

Essential Question
How are writers inspired by animals?

by Paul Mason
illustrated by Vladimir Aleksic

It was the last day of school. The bell rang for recess. Sal and his friends ran to the playground and shouted with joy.

Sal was excited. Tomorrow Sal and his uncle Mikey were going to their family cabin near Lake Lacuna.

Uncle Mikey and Sal liked to go fishing at Lake Lacuna, although they had to follow a no-technology rule at the cabin.

Sal's friend Ricky was surprised. "There's no TV in the cabin? No video games?" Ricky asked.

Sal shook his head. He replied, "No technology. It's the rule at the cabin."

Sal said, "There is an enormous catfish at the lake. It's called the Big One. It has lived there for a long time. I'm going to catch it this year."

Ricky wrinkled his nose. "Ugh, I don't like fishing. I'd rather play computer games."

The next morning, Uncle Mikey arrived in his truck. He waved at Sal with his arm outstretched.

"Do you want a cup of coffee?" Sal's dad asked.

Uncle Mikey replied, "Sure, but we're in a hurry. Sal and I want to get to the lake and start fishing."

During the trip to the cabin, Uncle Mikey and Sal had to shout over the noise of the truck. The truck grumbled like an old mule.

They arrived at the little town of Lacuna and stopped at Pete's General Store to get a few things.

The store owner, Pete, grinned when he saw Sal and Uncle Mikey. The shelves behind Pete were filled with supplies.

"Well, <u>look what the cat brought in</u>. I haven't seen you guys in a while," Pete said.

> **In Other Words**   look who is here. En español, *look what the cat brought in* quiere decir *mira quién llegó*.

Uncle Mikey shook Pete's hand. "Sal and I are staying at our family cabin for a few days."

Pete said, "The fishing's not very good at the moment."

"What about the Big One?" Sal asked.

Pete chuckled. "Do you think you can catch the Big One, Sal? No one's managed to catch it yet."

Pete asked Sal, "How do you plan to catch the fish?"

"I'll put very smelly bait on my fishing line. I read that catfish smell their prey," Sal answered.

"I have some smelly bait for sale," Pete said.

STOP AND CHECK

What is the Big One?

5

Chapter 2

A Break in the Line

fin

plaque

Sal and Uncle Mikey arrived at the family cabin. There was a plaque with a catfish above the fireplace. Sal's father had caught the catfish when he was a boy. The fish was large, but its fins looked old and brittle.

Sal thought, "If I catch the Big One, I can hang it above the fireplace, too."

Uncle Mikey and Sal walked to the dock. They saw several people fishing on the lake. Uncle Mikey and Sal put bait on their fishhooks. Then they threw their fishing lines into the water.

Language Detective The fish is the subject noun. Find another subject noun on this page.

"I love staying at the cabin," Uncle Mikey said. He looked at the family cabin in the woods. "You can thank your great-grandfather. He was the builder of the cabin."

Sal was surprised. Uncle Mikey continued, "Your great-grandfather wrote poems here. Some of his poems were published."

Suddenly Sal felt a tug on his fishing line. A fish was trying to eat the bait. Sal sat up and gripped the fishing rod.

"I've got a fish!" he gasped. The fish began to pull harder on the fishing line. Sal pulled the rod back, and the fishing line went slack. The fish had disappeared.

Uncle Mikey said, "The fishing line isn't strong enough. That fish must be enormous."

Language Detective   Builder is the predicate noun of the sentence. What is the subject noun?

Sal was disappointed, but he quickly tied a new hook onto the fishing line. Then he put the fishing line back into the water.

Sal and Uncle Mikey fished for the rest of the afternoon, but they didn't catch any fish.

The next day, they went to Pete's store and they bought stronger fishing line. They fished in different places, but they still didn't catch any fish.

Sal thought that maybe he should have stayed at home and played computer games with Ricky.

On the last night in the cabin, Sal knew he had only one more day to catch the Big One.

STOP AND CHECK

What did Sal's great-grandfather do?

The next morning, Sal and Uncle Mikey decided to fish at a place that Pete had recommended. The water was as smooth as glass. Sal and Uncle Mikey cast their fishing lines into the water.

Sal hoped a fish would appear. Suddenly he felt a pull on the fishing line.

Sal yelled, "I've got something!" His fishing rod bent, and the fishing line pulled tight. A fish was taking the bait. Sal started to <u>wind in</u> the line.

In Other Words pull in. En español, *wind in* quiere decir *enrollar*.

fishing rod

stool

lake

bobber

reel

cattails

rock

fishing line

Uncle Mikey said, "Wait until the fish stops dragging the fishing line. Then wind in the line."

Sal could feel the fish tugging on the line. The fish was trying to escape.

Then the fish stopped moving, and Sal started to wind in the fishing line. The fishing rod bent as the fish struggled to get away again.

In a flash, Sal saw a dark tail and a white belly. The fish was struggling. Sal's arms were getting very tired.

Uncle Mikey was ready to help, but Sal wanted to catch the fish by himself.

Sal pulled the fishing rod up and back. Then he wound in more of the fishing line. The fish pulled away. Sal could sense the fish was exhausted.

The fish was splashing at the surface of the water. Its tail was flapping. It was a catfish! Sal knew he had beaten the fish. He continued to wind in the fishing line.

Uncle Mikey yelled, "Wow, that's a monster!" He helped Sal get the fish into shallow water. Sal had a huge grin. He was sure the catfish was the Big One.

STOP AND CHECK

Describe how Sal caught the catfish.

The fish had a huge head and long whiskers. Its skin was the color of cold steel. The fish flopped in the shallow water. Its mouth was opening and shutting.

Uncle Mikey said, "I can't believe it! You caught the Big One!"

Sal looked at the Big One. Sal didn't think he should keep the fish. The catfish was old, and it had lived in the lake for many years.

"Quick, Uncle Mikey, take some pictures with your camera," Sal said. "Then I'm going to put the fish back in the lake."

fin

hook

whisker

13

Uncle Mikey took some photographs of the fish. Then he pulled the hook out of the fish's mouth.

Sal and Uncle Mikey put the Big One into deep water. The fish flopped around, then disappeared beneath the surface of the water.

They packed up and stopped at Pete's store before they drove home.

Pete said, "Well, you didn't catch anything all week, and then you caught the Big One. Good job, kid!"

camera

fishing vest

paper

desk

"I'll send you a picture to put on your wall," Uncle Mikey said.

"Thanks," Pete said, smiling.

On the way home, Sal thought about the battle with the Big One. The photographs would prove that Sal had caught the big fish. But Sal knew the photographs wouldn't tell the whole story.

"Maybe I could follow in my great-grandfather's footsteps," Sal thought. He could be creative and write a descriptive poem. His poem would tell about the time Sal caught a legend but let it live.

STOP AND CHECK

Why did Sal let the Big One live?

Respond to Reading

Summarize

Use important details to summarize *The Big One*. Your graphic organizer may help you.

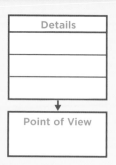

Text Evidence

1. How do you know that *The Big One* is realistic fiction? **GENRE**

2. Who tells this story? What tells you this? **POINT OF VIEW**

3. What kind of description is "grumbled like an old mule" on page 4? **FIGURATIVE LANGUAGE**

4. Write a description of the Big One that Sal could have written. Use pronouns such as *I*, *me*, and *my* to show what Sal thinks and feels. **WRITE ABOUT READING**

Compare Texts

Read some haiku that were inspired by animals.

Peacock

Royal peacock struts,

Proud tail spreads, a cloak of blue.

"Look at me," he says.

Grass Snake

Snake lying on stone,

Curled up like a dark ribbon,

Stealing the sun's rays.

Robin

Robin picks through leaves,

A dancer in red clothing,

Seeking out his lunch.

Make Connections

What might have inspired the poet to write the haiku *Robin*? **ESSENTIAL QUESTION**

How do animals inspire the writers of *The Big One* and the haiku? **TEXT TO TEXT**

Focus on Genre

Poetry Haiku are short poems. A haiku has three lines. The first line has five syllables. The second line has seven syllables. The third line has five syllables. Writers often use figurative language such as simile and metaphor to describe something in a haiku.

Read and Find Each haiku in the Paired Read is inspired by an animal. In *Grass Snake*, the writer uses a simile ("like a dark ribbon"). In *Peacock*, the writer uses a metaphor ("tail … a cloak"). Reread the haiku *Robin*. Look for a simile or a metaphor. How does this simile or metaphor help to describe the animal?

Your Turn

With a partner, choose a photograph or illustration of an animal. Use this picture to help you write a haiku. Write three lines that describe the animal. Then shorten each line until you find the best way to describe the animal. Try to use a simile or metaphor to describe the animal. Count the syllables in each line. Make sure you have used the correct number of syllables. Display the haiku you wrote next to the image of the animal that inspired you.